PUBLIC SCHOOL.

NORTH SIDE OF RIVERSIDE AVENUE.

GTON TERRITORY - 1884

THE ABRAMS STORY

William Abrams
London, England
1880

Clara Ciff Abrams
London, England
1880

THE ABRAMS STORY

HENRY L. REIMERS

YE GALLEON PRESS
FAIRFIELD, WASHINGTON
1977

Library of Congress Cataloging in Publication Data

Reimers, Henry L. 1909-
The Abrams story.

1. Abrams, William, 1836-1920. 2. Spokane--Biography.
3. Pioneers-Washington (State)--Spokane--Biography. I. Title.
F899.S7A257 979.7'37 (B) 78-5584
ISBN 0-87770-181-4

The Abrams Story

WILLIAM ABRAMS: GLOBE-TROTTING PIONEER

William Abrams was born in the Salisbury region of England in 1836. Aside from this fact his family knew almost as little about his early years as was known about the origin of the massive and mysterious structure known as Stonehenge, surely a familiar sight to his youthful eyes. Even less would have been realized about this remarkable man had he not, in late years, devoted two lengthy evenings to reciting his experiences. Surely an adventure saga well worth preserving might at that time have been recorded, but fathers can be taken for granted by those closest to him, and there would be chances later on to re-check certain events of continuing interest. Unfortunately such was not the case, therefore this recounting can only be a miniscule portion of the experiences of a man who was certainly a globe-trotter par-excellence, one who saw world acclaimed excitement at its highest, and often encountered human nature at its lowest. Only the rarest and most unlikely infusion of good fortune can ever complete the gaps in this narrative.

Since his mother occupied the responsible position of Post-mistress, with its opportunity for stability and modest financial security, it is highly probable that William Abrams received a better than average education for those times. This is subtantiated by noting the books that accompanied him on his travels, volumes by Scott, Dickens, Bulwer-Lytton, and always "The Good Book". Not content to be an "armchair adventurer", it remained for his energy, integrity, and tendency to straight talk to take him far, and among men who respected only those others who demonstrated from the start an ability and desire to stand on their own feet. In that distant day when "the sun never set on the British Empire" a host of young men set forth to various corners of that realm, seeking fortunes, business opportunities, family recognition, or merely adventure in whatever guise it awaited them.

British mercantile enterprises, such as Hudson's Bay and the East India Companies offered occupation to those with the needful training, to say nothing of recognized "pull". Army commissions were available at a price, for the price of empire meant an urgent need for military force, where and when needed. It is unlikely that the latter had any influence on William Abram's first venture away from merry old England, but there may have been prospects of employment in India, when at the age of 18 he boarded a ship bound for that sub-continent. Quite likely he earned his passage, for he was ambitious, and the family income which provided a comfortable living would scarcely have enabled him to travel in luxury. His departure deprived him of a chance to get into the Crimean War, as things developed, but risk of life and limb was not entirely eliminated.

Embarkation was probably from Southampton, thence to the Azores, the Canary Islands and on around the great bulge of West Africa, with the occasional sighting of skulking vessels suspected of slave trading, and stops at various ports to dispatch mail, freight, and passengers, who may have shuddered at the prospect of spending years in some abysmal coastal settlement as a trading post employee. William Abrams doubtless cast ahead in his imagination and wondered if India would provide brighter prospects. There was a welcome stopover at Cape Town, then the proud possession of the Boers, a place that was inviting in its own way had he not been previously committed. All too soon the voyage resumed, and what had once been known as "the Stormy Cape" proceeded to show it could still live up to that ancient name. A terrific storm arose which battered the clumsy steamer.

Hastening on an errand below decks young Abrams was halted by an appealing voice and a desperate grasp on his arm. The elderly lady, terrified as to expression, but fighting to be calm had some sage advice:

"Young man, if you have never prayed before pray now!"

The point was probably well taken, and perhaps incorporated into certain other official duties, or possibly many other minds were seized with the same idea, at any rate the craft weathered the "blow" and rounded the Cape of Good Hope to Port Elizabeth. Some repairs were in order and during this time there was opportunity to briefly explore the hinterlands. This part of Africa tempted but had to be resisted at that time for India still awaited. In time the boat pushed on to Madagascar, thence across the Indian Ocean to touch at Bombay. Much of what William Abrams saw was uninviting, especially the prevalence of poverty and disease. A relative few lived in opulence and closed their eyes to the misery of the least fortunate.

It was many weeks before southern India could be passed and journey's end at Calcutta reached. This might as well never have come to pass. A cholera epidemic was raging and had claimed sister Sarah and the brother-in-law he had not seen for many years, and whose presence in this vast colony had inspired him to seek a future here. There was nothing to hold him now, and strong inducement to journey elsewhere, anywhere. The same ship took him on to Rangoon and then Singapore. This telling seems to abbreviate the time of travel, which actually required many months. In the Asiatic ports there was no premium on hustle and bustle; unloading and lading of cargo was prolonged and deliberate.

It seemed a smile from Lady Luck when a chance came to secure a berth on an Australia-bound freighter. This was land more to the choosing of an Englishman, with a climate that was sure to be a relief from that of the tropics. Being familiar with Captain Cook's voyages of discovery there and elsewhere made the small continent seem like a touch of home, something to look forward to while coasting along Sumatra, Java and western Australia to harbor at Fremantle. Here it seemed representatives of every nation and race teemed along the docks and in the crowded streets, and all the talk was of "Gold!"

William Abrams had heard and read of California's frenzied gold rush of 1849, and for several years following, and now he met veterans of that historic occasion. Actually Australia had contributed a noted collection of salty individuals to that event, the so-called "Sidney Ducks", representing some of the riff-raff dumped on the small continent as one step in England's penal policy. Vigilante action had been necessary to suppress the violence in San Francisco, but this was no longer urgently needed. Now southwestern Australia was enjoying its own "gold rush" and the flow of population was in the direction of this newest lodestone. The name "Kalgoorlie" was on everyone's lips, a site many arid miles east of Fremantle and Perth, with transportation negligible and hardship rampant, with a crime wave in the offing, a dire hazard for the unwary.

Young Abrams, by virtue of his up-bringing, was not one to waste his wages on such dubious enticements as the various ports of call had offered. He was able to head for the "diggings" well-equipped with tools and supplies. It is likely he had companions, and good men, otherwise his chances of seeing Kalgoorlie would have been rather dim, traffic being what it was and Law what it wasn't. At about that same time in that place there was another colorful traveler, Ranald McDonald, a half-breed son of a Hudson's Bay Company Factor, educated to be a banker, but by choice a world adventurer. He has been described as the first American to visit Japan and live to tell about it, and it appears that a U.S. Naval officer transported him and others less known to history away from the Land of the Rising Sun following some tactful negotiations with Nippon. McDonald was far from though with adventuring and Australia's gold fields knew him. It seems possible that he and Abrams may have met and compared experiences. In that case it is the height of irony that they spent their last years in homes hardly 150 miles distant from each other.

In gold camps it was always first come, first served, and those who came late found the finest prospects claimed. This was not entirely bad, for if one was willing to work for one of the lucky ones his labor insured a better return than was enjoyed by those who continually sought a strike and went broke doing so. For many the thrill of "hitting it rich" was the climax. With a few pouches of dust they were ready to head for the big city. In such cases a good claim might be bought cheaply, since to go away for a while would result in it being "jumped". A trusted individual might be offered a chance to work it on shares but William must have seemed slightly young for such a responsibility. The day came when he took time off to prospect. There is some reason to believe that "beginner's luck" was with him, a problem in itself, for in the region there was a sizable collection of "hardcases" who were "hard up". California's brand of mining camp justice, which many of the inhabitants were acquainted with, had some influence in suppressing the overt criminality that might have been anticipated, and this was before Ned Kelly and the "bush rangers" had achieved full prominence. Actually the deadliest dangers were heat, dust, shortage of water, scarcity and expense of supplies, and a general environment that had to seem crude to one of civilized traditions. There is ample reason to believe that in deference to youth and this self-imposed exile, kindly fortune smiled favorably, possibly to the extent of at least one rich pocket, and in time our traveler was safely back in Perth, and if he was well off in the matter of gold, he was even more richly endowed with know-how that was involved in skimming wealth from the earth's surface, and this might be made to pay off in more favorable locations. Certainly Kalgoorlie had been a place to test one's mettle no matter what the reward in "dust," while Coolgardie and Ballarat gave no cause for complaint, considering the limited time spent there.

Again the knowledge of Captain Cook's Australian cruise and his voyage around the world had its influence. Why should not William Abrams extend his own travels to encircle the globe, though in a direction opposite to that of the doughty and heroic captain. It is an inference that his route took him to the ports on the continent's southern coast, thence to the northeast. He must have seen a multitude of South Sea Islands but it is to be hoped the itinerary avoided Tahiti. One of his rather strict up-bringing could scarcely have appreciated the hula dance as interpreted by the dusky maidens of that enchanted island. On the other hand, when he reached Hawaii it would be explained to him that there "the hands told the story." Probably Captain Cook's death site would have interested him more than grass skirts or grass huts.

San Francisco was the next port of call. He had heard much of this place from Kalgoorlians who had been there, so he was aware of the "Barbary Coast" and its fateful attractions-----and had the wisdom to avoid them. Besides he had no wish to squander his capital, but rather to increase it. Up in the Northwestern territories of the United States a series of new gold strikes were front page news in such papers as were available, Pierce, Colville, Bannack and Virginia City claiming the big share of newsprint. Boats heading north were crammed beyond the limits of safety but things would not soon improve. The first step was to reach Portland, Oregon, and though saddle horses were available for a ride up well-established trails William Abrams was Briton enough to prefer the high seas; besides the water route was quicker. Crossing the bar at Columbia River's mouth proved hazardous as that all but forgotten storm near South Africa, and Portland proved to be a rather squalid collection of crude housing desperately trying to rise from the forests. There was surely nothing to attract a prolonged stay and steamboats were ready to carry him on up-stream.

The first leg of such a journey as he now contemplated would take him to the Cascades, a stretch of falls and white water that was still greedy after claiming the lives of uncounted immigrant settlers. A portage railroad moved traffic around the rapids and another steam boat offered passage to The Dalles, as bleak a spot as any he had seen since departing Australia. This place was a "man-trap", designed to plunder the well-heeled traveler headed inland, and to relieve the outward bound trekker of any wealth he might have obtained at the diggings. Having survived eight years of being "on his own" in the out-reaches of civilization, Abrams could read the signs, and all unscathed he traveled the portage around Celilo Falls and embarked on a steamboat that could take him to Lewiston, Idaho, at this season of the year. At Wallula he was tempted to get off and take the stage to turbulent Walla Walla, the gateway City as far as the Idaho and Montana gold camps were concerned. When he learned that snow in the mountains would block the farther end of that route he stayed aboard as the vessel moved into the Snake River and battled its way up that turbulent stream.

At what is familiarly known as Lyon's Ferry there was a stop while some mules and baggage were unloaded on the north bank. A crew of packers intended to take the Mullan Trail from there, with a hefty load of supplies to bargain off at whatever gold camp was easiest to reach. After the harsh winter that had visited the Northwest all provisions would be in demand. It would have been possible to accompany this group by paying for a share of provisions and helping out where needed but in the end it seemed better to go by boat as far as possible. In this case that meant Lewiston, and then several miles up the Clearwater River toward Orofino. This was a favored camp, weatherwise, but living costs were high. It proved advisable to take a job and see if placer mining in America was comparable to Australian methods.

Belatedly the snow relaxed its grip on the mountains and it was possible to move higher up to Pierce, a settlement which had mushroomed on land claimed by the Indians as a treaty right, and which was a source of anger to the tribesmen. Here another stint of work was in order before experienced mountaineers pronounced that travel over Lolo Pass should be possible. It was necessary to hire a packer to haul the needed supplies over the precarious route where Lewis and Clark's expedition had nearly perished from hunger almost in sight of their goal. The packer and his helper had charge of a lengthy string of animals that tramped a path through the remaining drifts, but often downed timber barred the way, or small landslides had wiped out the footing. At such times everyone wielded axe, saw, pick or shovel. Second thought might have brought regret for the choice made at Lyon's Ferry, but ruing past decisions was not a characteristic of Mr. Abrams. More than a week was logged before the rugged trail gave way to easier travel down Lolo Creek and into the Bitterroot Valley. Everyone was pleased except the boss packer, whose animals were now more lightly loaded. Some of his cargo had been oats for the mules, since adequate pasture had not been counted on at that season. They turned along the valley to the nearest trading post, hoping to sell what supplies were left, or else buy enough more to justify a trip on to Virginia City.

From there on the trip was comparatively easy, though it was necessary to buy a saddlehorse. Tramping on foot over the Lolo Trail could be done as swiftly as the pack critters moved, but on the better going the horses stepped out, past the site where gold had first been found in Montana Territory, past a rugged butte so underlaid with copper that within the space of a few years it would be a source of great wealth and disputation, beyond Deer Lodge and on to Alder Gulch, where short months before one Bill Fairweather had panned the gravel to reveal the richest gold deposits known up to that time. Virginia City and Nevada City were roistering, festering locales exhibiting the customary abandon of such "boom" towns, but slightly subdued as a hard-bitten Vigilante corps had taken drastic action toward the renegades and "road agents" who had plundered the region unhindered from the time of the first strike. William Abrams was probably on the scene when Joseph Slade was executed, mainly on the charge of being a "nuisance". This example of frontier action must have been startling, since at Kalgoorlie the offense would have been punishable by banishment. It was a thing the Vigilantes would never point to with pride regardless of the therapeutic value it may have effected on any "hard cases" still lingering in the camps.

The days of simple surface operations were on the decline. Eventually dredges would take over the task of making a final "clean-up" and when that was over Alder Gulch would no longer justify such a name. Long before then Mr. Abrams had departed, probably north by way of Helena to Fort Benton, still a fur trading post of some importance. There steamboat passage down the Missouri was available. Moving swiftly downstream, the craft passed many wood-cutter camps where fuel was corded neatly to supply the vessels laboring up the river against the powerful current. Going down fewer stops were needed, which was just as well, since wily Sioux and Crow raiding parties often wiped out the wood-cutters and lay in wait for any lax boat crew that tied up near shore. Eventually St. Louis was reached, still a great fur market, and here another steamboat took him up the Ohio, still the "Beautiful River" its Indian name implied.

At Pittsburg there must have been opportunity to travel on eastward by stagecoach, or by train. Thc lattcr might have tempted, since Englishman George Stephenson was responsible for the invention of the locomotive, but cars were crowded. The effects of the Civil War, only slightly known as to detail in the western camps, was now everywhere apparent. It would have been like William Abrams to fare north by some means and complete his trip to New York by way of the Erie Canal. Canal use was well established in Britain but this one had achieved great renown, not all of it lauditory, judging by the pen of Charles Dickens, who rode the length of the famed waterway and found little to praise in the way of passenger accommodations. For one enured to the sterner ways of life the trip was surely not without interest and modest comforts for that time.

At last in New York, bustling and burgeoning from the impact of the Civil War and the commerce engendered by the Erie Canal, an Englishman might have been ill at ease. His country had abolished slavery years previous, and made stern efforts to stamp out the African slave trade, which was all to the good. At the same time, because cotton from the South was all-important to the British textile industry, some favoritism was displayed toward the Confederacy. The fortunes of war were gradually tilting toward the North, however. Whether Mr. Abrams booked passage to England from New York, or from a Canadian port, the last lap of his journey around the world soon terminated in "Blighty", perhaps in the harbor at Southampton, from where he had set sail originally. It can only be hoped that his mother was still alive to welcome him home, but he had been absent for a decade, and then as now, world events moved swiftly, and the youth who had departed returned a mature, self-possessed and experienced man, who may soon have found English home life very confining, with no outlet for the talents he had developed during long years abroad.

By a quirk of fate something akin to the turn of fortune related in the story "Acres of Diamonds" had transpired during the lengthy globe-trotting years. South Africa, comparatively handy to a venturesome Briton, had become a land of opportunity, where young men might establish large plantations or engage in mining. Even a noteworthy gold strike had taken place at Johannesburg about 1860. Recalling how tempting that country had seemed on that early voyage, William Abrams lost little time in arranging his affairs and re-embarking. In time he found himself once more at Port Elizabeth busy with plans to journey north to the scene of the most recent strike. Since he was of independent means he did not have to settle for laboring on the claims of others. Actually there was little opportunity, for natives were available for these tasks.

How many prospecting junkets he undertook and how much time was involved cannot be ascertained. Even his comfortable means must have been taxed severely but finally he "struck it". The strike was a reasonably good one, well worth developing, since Kaffirs were available to handle the extensive operations. The returns far exceeded anything in his previous experience. At night the natives huddled close in camp, while the roaring of lions outside the circle of firelight played havoc with sound sleep. One night William Abrams was awakened from uneasy slumber by the awareness of questing fingers probing cautiously about his body seeking a money belt. Very wisely the intended victim "froze" and groped for escape from the impasse. Actually the coup, if carried to conclusion, would yield a good haul, one not to be surrendered tamely, but resistance would bring a smash from brass knuckles or a stabbing knife. Give a word of credit to those same pestiferous lions. Their sudden outburst, seeming to come from the midst of the drowsing Kaffirs brought the natives to their feet with frantic shouts of alarm and a mad rush toward the protection of the "baas." The foiled culprit quickly drew back and slunk away into the darkness, choosing to gamble with the king of beasts out there rather than face the wrath of the outraged white man.

Wild game contributed to the sustenance of laborers and the venture proved so profitable that when diamond mining began to steal some of the glamor from the gold camps, about 1870, it was possible to resist a temptation to have a look at Kimberly—for the time being.

William Abrams remained on his claims and worked them for enough years to put the name of Abram's Gulch permanently on the map of Africa. There came the time when the digging had to be extended far below the surface and this called for techniques and an increased labor force, factors with which he chose not to contend, and resulted in a sale of the property for a sum which, added to his other returns, should have provided for a lifetime of leisure. Then it was time to investigate the diamond fields but there was no real drive to accumulate more wealth there, though in light of later developments it would have been nice to unearth at least one choice gem. This latest prosperity may have induced him to take the long way home and so complete a second journey around the world. A treasured picture is of the S. S. Garonne, a combination steam and sail vessel on which he returned on the "last trip from Australia". This memento originated in Gravesend, a short distance from London. This time he would see the "capital of Empire", and doubtless a goodly share of his money had been forwarded to a London bank.

S.S. "GARONNE.

William Abrams completed his second trip around the world on this ship.

Back in England he learned that his former gold property was doing very well for the new owners. It might be said that a fortune had thereby slipped through his hands, but he had plenty of substance to show for nearly a decade and a half on the Dark Continent. Rather than mull over the whimsies of fate, which seldom provide real satisfaction, Mr. Abrams arranged for a long delayed visit to London. Whether he found its reality on a par with descriptions in his favored literature can only be conjectured. He did find romance, and to a staid, responsible gentleman in his early forties, this eclipsed anything else the sprawling, congested old city had to offer, be it Westminster Abbey, the old Norman tower, the Crown Jewels, or the ghastly "stews" where the poor thronged and strove as best they knew how to survive in the face of continual poverty, disease and crime. The attractions of Britain, Scotland, Ireland and Wales were likewise banished and 18 year old Clara Ciff monopolized his complete attention. Her family numbered 15 children, dependent for what must have been a precarious existence on the father's employment as a groom. For him work must have been plentiful, but certainly offered no sinecure, and doubtless the youthful Clara often thought of a more spacious and gracious way of life.

It need not be thought that so sizable a family lived at a poverty level, not if the energy and ambition of this particular daughter was typical. There must have been work within the powers of the older sons and daughters which contributed to the livelihood of all while they remained at home, and back of all this was a supplementing pride that refused to bow to circumstances. Clara was always able to think of her mother's people, the Treachers, with satisfaction, likewise her father's family, the Ciffs, both with lengthy traditions. Also a hint that there might be some kinship with the Rothchilds helped buoy her spirits as she bustled about at her housekeeping chores and the endless sewing that was instrumental in keeping up appearances. If she entertained girlish hopes of a Prince Charming coming to offer a fairer domain it is not to be wondered at, but the great event in her life betokened little of the fairy tale character.

She was practical and ambitious. This led to work in a restaurant where the kindly cook each night filled a basket with "left-overs" to take home as a supplement to the household provisions. This boon was appreciated, and the job as well, for the pay could then be stretched to afford night school. This is a clue to her nature, also to that of the parents, since education was not compulsory and working children usually contributed their pittance to the family exchequer. This experience opened the window to a wider horizon, — but a window is not a door.

Daughter Louisa points to this in a biographical note. "When she (Mother) was young there were few opportunities for girls in the business world; but with education and training she, being of pleasant demeanor, might have made a good receptionist. Also, her penchant for neatness and orderliness would have stood her well with employers similar to some of the ones I have known.

"I think her best bet would have been as a nurse. With proper training I am sure she would have been an excellent one."

In the light of later developments a certain business insight and that definite talent for nursing were only awaiting the proper opportunity.

Aside from the previously mentioned "fringe benefits" such as the left-over basket and the unfailing kindness of the generous cook, the restaurant position left something to be desired. The dining room was a private one for the exclusive use and convenience of high officials, railroad VIP's, whose class awareness did not deter them from directing amorous glances and unwanted attention toward the girl employees, a situation not to be tolerated.

Then ensued a more prosaic occupation as an efficient maid in the boarding house run by the eminently respectable Mrs. Evans. One of the residents there could have been Mr. William Abrams, who would surely have met busy Clara in the normal routine of her employment. Fate! What followed was an attraction of opposites; a man who thought people should be satisfied to remain members of the class into which they had been born, and a girl who ardently believed people were entitled to the greatest heights within reach of their initiative, talents and ambition. Later there were introductions to all the household. The father, whose work as a groom may have been supplemented by renting rigs or driving a "fare" on business trips about the city, could not have failed to be impressed, though that was not too essential in that strong-willed family. It followed that the acquaintance between Mr. Abrams and Clara developed, even though they were poles apart age-wise, he a sober, solid citizen of the world, not given to impulse, while she was alert, eager to be up and doing. It would have been contrary to his nature for William to reveal his ample means but his bearing must have revealed that this was no run-of-the-mill man. Probably he related his various experiences in the course of dinners and frequent visits, possibly in greater detail than he ever did again, for the restricted life of these people made them an appreciative audience. Actually this recounting of adventure was primarily for the benefit of a certain one, and the young lady must have been as enthralled as any, since the social outcasts of Kalgoorlie and Kaffirs of Africa were at a safe distance geographically and time-wise, and storms at sea need have no fears for one who was content to look upon the Thames from London Bridge. As for disease and the deaths accompanying the well-nigh perpetual pestilences, one could keep in mind that "cleanliness was next to Godliness," and by avoiding the slums there was hope of evading typhoid, diptheria, the plague, and of course Asiatic Cholera. Clara listened, and sooner than might have been supposed, she heard something that required an answer. Young as she was, and inexperienced, the question could not have been a complete surprise. Her mother would surely have seen the proposal coming, and implied approval, and this the father would have seconded, justifying his earlier expectations. A good, early marriage was desirable when a man numbered several daughters. The answer, of course, was "yes."

It seems likely that the marriage ceremony was elaborate enough to please the youthful bride and demonstrate the substance of her responsible husband. This was followed by a honeymoon at Brighton, the popular mecca for all newly-weds of that era. It is unlikely that the age discrepency caused any second glances for in England there was always a certain practical point of view to be considered, and greater variance in years for lesser reasons was common enough. As for the couple, neither realized that this would probably be the lengthiest tour they would take together, in their native land. For William Abrams it was ironic to know so much of the world and so little of his own country, a condition he was not to improve upon.

One thing became clear. There was little opportunity in Britain for Mr. Abrams. His experience qualified him well for one activity, surface mining. Clara doubtless enjoyed the scale of living he was about to provide but even his resources could not guarantee an extended span of such living. Another sobering note was added when Edith, the first child, died in infancy, from one of the prevalent ailments which posed a constant threat to the very young. No fine assortment of presents bestowed on the young wife could begin to compensate for such a loss. It is possible, too, that her family received some form of endowment from time to time, prompted by generosity rather than urgency. For William Abrams big city living must have palled after a matter of months, and he began to restlessly scan the horizon. Another daughter, Lucy, born in 1882, kept the couple in England for a while longer but meanwhile the future was charted. Clara may not have been entirely happy as the plan was unfolded, satisfied as she was to be surrounded by people, but the young lady had an abundance of nerve and courage for one of her comparatively small stature, and she may have welcomed a chance for adventure and life in a new sphere, within limitations.

To Lord Selkirk must go some credit for introducing British colonists to Canada's vast territory. His protegees were settled in the Red River region of Manitoba and there was friction almost from the start. The Metis, or mixed bloods, had developed homes and property there decades before the influx began. Under the leadership of Louis Riel they resisted being forced from land which they deemed theirs by right of occupation and use. There was furor and bloodshed before the uproar was decided, and even then justice was not completely served. The uprising of previous years was well known to William Abrams, but he envisioned emigration to Saskatchewan, far west of the recently troubled area, which similar trouble was not anticipated.

Leave taking could not have been easy, the wife from parents and numerous relatives, the husband from older brother John, with whom he had finally become well-acquainted. John had left home before the other was born, and there had been much to catch up on, but now both men realized when the seas parted them this time there would be little likelihood of another meeting.

The Abrams Story

William and Clara Abrams probably dis-embarked at Toronto after an uneventful voyage, though this first ocean crossing must have loomed more impressively where the wife was concerned. Railroad transportation was available to Regina, and there team, wagon and equipment were purchased to help launch an ambitious farming project far to the north, where 320 acres had been obtained. This land must have been acquired at bargain rates, if indeed it cost anything, for Canada needed settlement just as had the United States when the Homestead Law was passed, to help fill up the western territories. Tilling the soil, of course, was a new endeavor for William Abrams, but he was adaptable and learned by observing his neighbors, as had been the case in mining. He did not stint on the hours employed and must have known an inward pride when his family was properly sheltered and the fertile acres began yielding to the plow. The move to Canada, had been a matter of some expense, and outfitting for proper farming must have been even more of a financial drain on one who believed in "paying as you go". The first crop would retrieve all of this outlay, however, and prospects were good, to his inexperienced eye. His wife had even learned to knead bread dough, after many lessons from him in the method he had mastered during years in "the diggings," or so he thought. Actually Clara had one day become so frustratd with the chore she flung the offending mixture full-force against the cabin wall. In the process of salvaging and restoration the "knack" developed and bread baking became an art. Dame fortune, whose smiles had been so favorable during his previous years, chose at this time to bestow her favors elsewhere, though Clara was the first to know.

Life on the broad prairie would have been lonely had Mrs. Abrams not been quite occupied with her child and the multiplicity of tasks incident to establishing a suitable home. There was little time for neighboring, due to the distance between homes, and much attention had to be applied to preparation for the bitter winters, whose perils lost nothing in the accounts they had heard. There was so little visiting that the arrival of an aged Indian was a welcome event to the lady of the house. It speaks well of Clara's bravery and intuition that she knew how to greet this elderly stranger and show the right degree of hospitality. Food, supplemented by tea or coffee, paved the way to friendship and confidence. The old chap became a frequent visitor, who always carried away gifts of sugar, flour, or the ingredients of his favorite beverages. He seemed a far cry from those who once before had joined in the Red River outbreak.

There came a day when the leathery native arrived in something of a hurry and shambled to the door. Clara met him, prepared with the usual greeting, but was given no time as the Indian broke out with a spate of excited words.

"So many moons and then—woo-oo—". With a grimy fore-finger the red man traced circles about his own graying head and the pantomime of scalping was horribly plain to even one as green as the young housewife. There was scarce an opportunity to stammer words of appreciation before the Indian departed. For this awesome information he wanted no gift. Perhaps this even meant he was joining other tribesmen in the impending depredation. The remaining hours of the day dragged with nerve-wracking slowness until William Abrams returned, to a storm of excitement and terrified outburst.

In all probability William Abrams had "spoiled" his young wife and deferred to her wishes when at all reasonable. Now he was put to the test. There was no reasoning away the fear, and even his stoical disposition could envision the Red River havoc being visited upon this region. His experience among the Kaffirs in Africa had schooled him in dealing with one type of native but the history of the New World had taught him that the worst had happened all-too-often. He deliberated the problems involved as thoroughly as the tenseness in the prairie home allowed. To pull out now would mean a real financial set-back. Any sale would be at a sacrifice, if indeed it was right to put his place on the block in the face of impending massacre, for surely others must have been similarly warned. He was not given as much time to think as might have been desired.

"You can stay if you want to", declared Clara, "but I'm taking Lucy and leaving as quick as I can. We're not waiting to be butchered".

That was how it was to be. The Abrams departed from their land with only what could be hauled in a single wagon, and traveled south to the United States boundary. They kept silent on their loss by making the move, but gave their reason for leaving to those who were interested. This met with pitying smiles from the few neighbors, and scoffing rejoinders as they left the threatened region farther behind. There was to be no more attempt to settle in Canada. Instead they sold everything except keepsakes and possessions that could be shipped by train, and climbed aboard, California bound. There were noteworthy sights aplenty but passage through Yuma, Arizona was notable for the horrendous heat. It was difficult to keep the baby's bottle of milk from curdling, there being no refrigeration available. William had some recollection of the San Francisco he had visited many years before, but now it lacked magnetism. The place chosen as a temporary residence was Pasadena, and there daughter Florence was born in December, 1883.

California did not hold the family for long, and why is a good question. The best guess is that useful employment was lacking, and the type of agriculture was so different that a farm venture seemed to entail a risk that could no longer be assumed. Within months all were in Seattle, whether by boat, train or stagecoach is uncertain, as are the waypoints that may have been investigated. Land in plenty, and reasonably priced, was available in the Puget Sound city, which was vainly struggling to arise from the smother of mighty forests and assume a role of prominence in the Northwest. Numerous logging and mill enterprises seemed inadequate to make a dent in the dense, dense growth. The future here looked distant indeed, and fraught with man-killing labor, yet something told Clara that a real opportunity was waiting here. Perhaps the mighty waters of Puget Sound, and the English named landmarks along it, was compensation for the broad Thames back home. She urged her husband to invest here, and surely there was very serious discussion. So much for woman's intuition, or was it a certain business inclination, previously mentioned, that prompted. The country of big trees had no charm for William, but if the Klondike Gold Rush and the "boom" it created in Seattle had been foreseen, he would have adjusted to circumstances, as had been so often done in the past, and been in contact with the third big "stampede" of his career, only a few years later. But nothing hinted to *him* of *gold*.

Instead, very soon attention was focused on a region east of the Cascade Mountains where the hopeful settlement of Spokan Falls was booming itself as the heart of a new "promised land". This last description may have sounded like an omen to one whose reliance on "the Good Book" had for the last couple of years been sternly tested, and the decision to seek a future fortune there was made as quickly as the resolve to avoid misfortune in Canada had been arrived at. The journey across the mountains could have been by stagecoach, but with two small children and the remaining personal possessions to consider, train travel was again resorted to.

The passage was somewhat roundabout, it being necessary to ride south to Portland, Oregon, and then parallel the Columbia River. William Abrams pointed out interesting sites remaining in memory from his earlier travels. Their significance was lost when newspapers from a "Candy Butcher" revealed that the threatened outbreak in Saskatchewan had actually come to pass. Once more it was natives battling against an inroad of settlers that destroyed or drove away the game and forced the Indians farther north into formidable and barren terrain. Joining in the fray were the mixed bloods, or Metis, sometimes regarded as "squatters", whose land claims were being disputed or re-arranged as the result of surveys and revised land policies. Against these aroused and desperate allies were the combined forces of the Mounted Police, ineffectual civilian groups and militia, plus several thousand soldiers. There was great fear that Indians from the United States would cross the boundary and unite with their fellows in an attempt to exterminate all whites in that section of Canada. This event is commonly known as "The Northwest Rebellion", or "Riel's Rebellion", but it seems to have started independently of this man's leadership, and when he was summoned the affair was beyond the power of any one individual to control. At first the "rebels" achieved marked success, resulting in the taking of many hostages, and a deplorable death toll of former friends and neighbors, just how many was never determined.

Regret for such a tragedy deleted most of the glamor from that trip through the Columbia Gorge and over fringes of the Columbia Basin and Palouse Country to the Northern Pacific Depot at the settlement by the big falls. Later they would learn that Louis Riel paid the extreme penalty for his efforts in behalf of the Canadian natives and mixed bloods, and that the whole debacle ended in the usual futility, but by then other things would demand a major share of interest and attention.

Spokan Falls was buzzing with tall tales about the 1883 gold rush to Prichard Creek, no farther away than the Coeur d'Alenes. The boisterous camps of Eagle and Murray would be rife with news regarding successful prospectors, but "The man with the Midas Touch" assayed all rumors on the basis of previous experience and resisted any temptation the elusive yellow metal may still have provided. The gold mining simmered down after a brief hey-day, but a silver strike that presently followed expanded to bonanza proportions, providing mammoth fortunes for countless lucky miners and investors. After nearly a century the abundant returns continue.

William Abrams turned his back on any Coeur d'Alene

venture, which may have been a relief to Clara, who sensed a more substantial opportunity near at hand for a responsible family man.

She discovered land that was for sale in what is now Browne's Addition, plenty of it, at a price within their means. Life in the crude settlement was preferable to a repeat of lonely ranch existence such as that on Saskatchewan's broad spaces, but let us give positive credit to the intuition and practical acumen that foretold this ground as the key to advantages and a promising future for the children. Coeur d'Alene Park and its environment of palacial homes, many of them founded on mining fortunes, was not long in substantiating these convictions, not shared by her husband, who was sure "the falls" would never really prosper, and viewed Cheney, once the County Seat, as the town that would thrive.

Neither community became home. Not being an American citizen, William Abrams could not file on a homestead, which may have been just as well, since the best claims were soon taken in any area. Instead, he bought railroad land. Family records show that on June 4, 1884, from the Northern Pacific, for a price of $240, he obtained the N½ of NW¼ of Sec. 23, T26N, R 40 EWM, this being about 20 miles west and slightly north of Spokane Falls, where the Four Mound and Crescent countries merged. On this a building site was chosen, in a rather secluded swale and near an excellent spring. Though sheltered, it was some distance from the road, a disadvantage during seasons of snow and mud, with little chance to view traffic there as a "break" from monotony and loneliness, had there been time for such afflictions. It was not the happiest of choices for another reason. Short years before the Spokane Indians, thoroughly aroused, staged a great dance and pow-wow at the forks on Coulee Creek (now known as Camp Washington), demonstrating resentment over their treatment by the white government.

Near the later site of Whitman (Pine Grove) School, all of the alarmed settlers had promptly "forted up" until the trouble, which involved payment for some petty improvements which a native had erected on land of his own choosing, and then been forced to abandon in favor of a paleface. The ado was settled when the newcomer was pressured into paying for the property, and was no longer an issue when the Abrams family arrived.

An attractive house gave a needed sense of security, and other buildings were added gradually, barn, spring-house, wood-shed, machine-shed and granary. English folk responding to the pride of their own land would insist on starting Lilac bushes and apple trees, to go with a large, fertile garden tract. With his wife and two daughters to consider Mr. Abrams, now verging on 50, felt that these were things that would ensure their welfare in the long run. Get rich quick sagas, related about recurring Coeur d'Alene mineral discoveries, caused no second thought. He had weighed using the last of his substance to support the family in town and grubstake himself for a prospecting jaunt, and discarded the idea. For him the right time would have been during the first visit to the Northwest, on the day when he had been tempted to leave the

Newly sawed lumber was used to finish this pioneer home.

steamboat at Lyon's Ferry and join the packers for their trip north through Spokan Indian Country, which had long intrigued him, and on to the Coeur d'Alenes, where vast wealth waited to be unearthed. Then, when luck had been a reliable companion, his own pick and shovel might have been the ones to claim the first bonanza. Now, years later, there may have been a feeling of resignation, a "hunch" that Africa had represented high tide in his fortunes. Having put his hand to the plow, literally and figuratively, it was in his mind to make a go of this farming.

The rich soil of Saskatchewan had yielded to tillage readily; not so this new ground. Here a carpet of thick wool-grass resisted penetration by the best of breaking-plows. No sooner than the continuous ribbon of sod was turned over than a myriad of rocks conspired to oust the share from the earth that was probably only marginal on the average. Huge hidden boulders lay in hiding to bring team and plow to a jarring halt, breaking beam, eveners, harness, and wrenching forth occasionally the mild epithet of "bloody be dam". By the time 80 acres were brought into cultivation it is likely that Mr. Abrams shared the thoughts of most settlers of his time, that it was too bad the Indians had lost to Colonel Wright and thus been forced to give up such a forbidding expanse of territory to innocent whites who scarcely knew what they were getting in to. This time it was a case of "toughing it out", following the old homesteader's song regarding survival in the West;

"Take your plow and bust the sod,
Then for a crop just trust in God".

There was no better advice available, and the birth of a son, Bill, in 1885, was a good omen. In years to come he would "make a hand". So favorable an augury eventually led to the purchase of more railroad land, the SW¼ of Sec. 15, price $1080, and the S½ of NW¼ of Sec. 23, price $240, all in Spokane County, Township 26 N, Range 40 EWM, and now the Abram's holding totaled 320 acres, much of it awaiting development. Since the "new hand"

This log barn was located on neighboring Indian Prairie.

A view of the Abrams home showing a picket fence similar to the one that extended one-fourth of a mile north to protect the lane from snow drifts.

would be unable to contribute for several years Clara added outside labor to her housewife duties. It was grueling work but her efforts and insight proved valuable. As an example of this dedication, the family planned to join in a community social, a rare enough pleasure, but this lady from teeming London sensed that one of the mares would foal that evening. Her husband was willing to let Nature take its course; not so his wife. The outing was canceled and "first things came first," with satisfactory results, for a healthy colt was added to their livestock.

It is a strange thing that immigrants from class conscious countries of Europe took democracy more seriously than many native born Americans who might jealously uphold their property rights and talk politics so vehemently. The Abrams family showed unusual generosity in the matter of community betterment. At the southwest corner of the home tract was a church where his children could benefit from Sunday School, though it is said he never attended services there. At the northwest corner he gave land for the building of a store and post office which was occupied for years by genial, well-liked Jimmy Jones, probably the only non-citizen to ever serve as Postmaster. Jones was from Canada, so he and Mr. Abrams could talk over their comparative experiences there, and since his supply of hard candy seemed inexhaustible, popularilty with the youngsters was assured, for he gave good measure, often without pay. Freight wagons brought supplies from Spokan Falls to keep his small building well stocked. It was a going establishment for half a century, then was moved to another site where it now serves in a lesser capacity. How helpful this post office must have been can be judged from documents in 1896 listing Welch, at the top of the Eddy Grade leading down from Four Mound Prairie to the LaPray Bridge over Spokane River, as the nearest one, though it was closer than an Indenture dated 1889, when Deep Creek Falls was designated. The latter, however, is still on the map, but who can find even a trace of the pioneer settlement known as Welch?

The convenient Jimmy Jones store and post office.

At the northeast corner ground was donated for the Greenwood School, and if the southeast corner had not been back in the wilds toward Coulee Creek it doubtless would have been available for some enterprise. These contributions improved and enlivened the neighborhood and provided an outlet for Clara's ambitions, for additions such as these made life seem more civilized, and if they suffered by comparison with big city features they offered some buffer against loneliness and monotony, and three growing children left little time for nostalgia. There had been another baby, Ruth, born in 1887, but the infant's life was brief. Daughter Louisa's words tell of this:

"Florence told me that she remembered mother holding Ruth in her arms, beside the open oven door, trying to warm her as the spark of life was ebbing away. Florence could not have been more than four, if even that, at the time; but it made a lasting impression on her as mother was quietly sobbing with the dying babe in her arms".

The house William Abrams had constructed was probably more impressive in appearance than in actual comfort. It was spacious enough but lack of efficient insulation was a detriment, one shared by most settler's homes in that era. Located almost one quarter mile from the main road along a shallow draw that bisected the quarter section, it benefited by being situated where the blasts of winter could not strike with full force, though snow often piled in deep drifts and forced detours through the timber to reach the road, this despite an extensive picket fence construction that ran the entire length of the entry lane and was designed to prevent such inconvenience. The apple trees and lilac bushes flourished. In time the house was well-masked by a lilac hedge that was a distinguishing feature in the community, and the fruit trees did equally well. The couple planned and planted better than they knew. More than eighty years later the hedge was still blossoming annually, the apples still burdened the somewhat bushy trees, while seeds spread by squirrels and birds had resulted in stout

The Abrams farmstead included a garden and orchard.

seedlings growing down the draw, half-hidden by brush, but well-laden with worm-free apples. Hopefully this homesite had something reminiscent of distant Salisbury. All of this was accomplished by dint of much labor, but when in the evening he sat down with his pipe, which he called "my pleasure", it should have been with the feeling that he was making as much progress as those born to life on a farm. It could be the crowded hours left too little time for shaving, at least none of the children could remember ever having seen their father's chin, but beards were common enough and did not provoke comment, though they gave some indication of age.

The Indians never proved a source of danger after Abrams moved to their railroad land, but the neighborhood was troubled with more than a little "rustling" and horse thievery. Several miles north in the breaks along the Spokane River was located the "Devil's Gap", where horses stolen in the Colville Valley were held until exchanged for animals "lifted" from the Palouse region. The Colville creatures were taken south to eventual buyers, the Palouse nags went north to the big valley. It has been told that a band of horsemen came by and recruited William Abrams to ride with them. Perhaps his days in Virginia City were known. The men were gone for many hours, and very soon there was an exodus of footloose young men. It is likely that any vigilante action resulted only in serving "walking papers" but one of those who left was later nailed by Montana stockmen who were administering more drastic penalties for thieving.

The horsemen rode again many years later when a certain minister of dark complexion and southern persuasion began a series of services in the church, evangelistic in character and highly stimulating, especially when the good "brother" had been plentifully fortified in advance with a chicken supper. Cartoonists and "gag writers" have sought to stereotype farm folk as stolid, averse to emotion and not too impressionable, none of which hold true. Among those who listened to the oratory were many who felt inspired to roll in the aisles or between the pews. Some who came primarily to audit the sessions also went down, being socially inclined, or out of curiosity. One roguish farmer chanced to come in contact with a well-turned ankle, a thing unseen normally, and raised a cry of "Jesus is here! I feel him, I've got him." The grip which he fastened on the ankle produced an answering shout, "I've been seized by the Holy Spirit! Halleluyah!"

Such commotion did not disturb the community too much until the "evangelist" began counseling the wrought up congregations to disinherit their children and name him in their stead. This over-ripe tripe was swallowed whole by many listeners. Interspersed with this advice and the clarion call to "bring more chicken", was a stern admonishment to "banish pleasure from your lives". As an example, husbands were commanded to "go home and smash your organs". Buxom wives paled and hardy yeomen shuddered. The injunction became well-nigh all inclusive when it was extended to include violins, mandolins, and even harmonicas. Musical instruments, inherited, or obtained by stinting in the matter of necessities, were rightly treasured. They contributed much to "live entertainment" so shock and resentment naturally resulted. Even so, there were instances of yielding to this and other stringent demands.

Vigilantes hit the saddle once more, it is told, backed by auxiliaries in Model T cars, and citizens who continued to sponsor the sessions were promised, and received, snug coatings of tar and feathers if they carried out the commands of the "revivalist" who was rapidly assuming an egotistical importance.

The outrageous "goings on" ended abruptly when a party of the "disinherited", both men and women, made a sudden appearance at one of the meetings. When they went in the front door the good "brother" went out the back door and took French leave, or perhaps French-Canadian leave, for he snaked his way through the lush field of winter wheat near the church, made good his escape, and it was rumored he later came to the end of a rope north of the boundary.

That was enough man-made excitement for a while, unless one cares to count the financial "panics" that came along regularly, so that an occasional good crop would be greeted with low prices, and in other years frost, drouth, or rain during the prolonged harvest kept a farmer from getting too far ahead, but the seasons continued and the settlers hung on. Even in depressed times existence on a farm was better than being unemployed in a town. There was often a shortage of food, but usually it was variety that was lacking. One winter, after being reduced to cornbread and syrup for days some member of the family voiced a protest, futile though it was bound to be, since a rampaging blizzard had the entire region snow-bound. It remained for William Abrams to provide the spine-stiffening morale tightener.

"*I'm* not ashamed to eat cornbread and seerup before the whole world", he stoutly averred, but when the storm abated they all climbed in a bobsled, thickly bedded with straw and furnished with heated rocks, robes and a kerosene lantern, to go shopping. For the sake of "an outing" they chose to drive across the exposed country to Deep Creek and lay in a good supply of necessities at Otto Behm's store. It is hoped there were funds for a few luxuries, including some tobacco. Soon the roads were opened and once more the Jimmy Jones store was equal to the demands on it, and by now these were somewhat increased for the family had grown to include Bessie, born in 1888 and Walter, born in 1889.

When the first farming efforts began it was customary to fall plow the fields so they would retain the snow and other moisture, then plant spring wheat. This matured rather late, which explains the delayed harvest and the loss from rain. One neighbor, Joe Haynes, clever and energetic as the Biblical Noah, chose to haul rough lumber from the Knostman mill and put roofs over his stacks. There was no end of jeering at this extra expense, and then came unending downpours that ruined at least two-thirds of all unsheltered grain. Wise, or otherwise, Joe Haynes garnered 100 per cent of his crop, but was too busy thereafter to run around saying, "I told you so."

Eventually the once virgin soil became depleted and yields dropped from 25 bushels per acre to a paltry 10 and 12. A partial solution came in the form of "dry farming", which meant that half of the land was seeded to newly introduced winter wheat. The other half was plowed in the spring and moisture was conserved by harrowing after each rain as soon as weeds started. In September, after a fall rain, the new kind of wheat would be planted, to live under the winter snow and be ready to harvest in July or early August. The yields returned to 25 and 30 bushels, but there were disadvantages. Winds, blowing over those plowed, harrowed fields, called summer fallow, would pick up and move great burdens of dust, coming in clouds that blackened the sky, producing a gloom that brought cows from the pasture and sent chickens up to their roosts. These "dusters" were terrifying when first experienced, and left a mammoth chore of housekeeping in their wake. The three Abrams daughters had plenty to do at such times for Clara's standards were high.

Washington Territory became Washington State but this provided no panacea for agriculture. The big problem seemed a need for more land, since only half of one's arable ground was in production each year. As related, Mr. Abrams purchased 160 acres one-half mile west and after the rigorous routine of "breaking" about 100 acres were brought under the plow. The soil was almost too good, sub-irrigated and so damp it was difficult to till, but in time this place contributed its fair share to the family weal. The home ranch, also rounded out to 160 acres, supplied another 100 arable acres. Binding, sometimes heading, then use of of a stationary thresher was the usual harvesting operation, all involving plenty of labor and wages. The boys, Bill and Walter, often wanted to help a neighbor and pocket some money so daughter Bessie filled in and thought it no hardship, finding her father companionable and considerate, while in the house her older sisters had to do everything just so, be it cleaning, cooking, or sewing. There was also a third son, Percy, born in 1895, whose

"Progressive farming" once meant early summer fallowing.

care received full attention. Mrs. Abrams believed in a "taut ship", and after upbringing in the household that numbered 15 at the time of her marriage, with more to follow, her goal was doubtless achieved. William, brought up like an "only child" in his home, had found the scurry and scamper of the youthful Ciffs rather entertaining, and would have settled for a less exacting regime.

Though it may not have occurred to them, the family was located in the heart of an international settlement, almost a duplicate of what had been left so far behind. To the east Joe Haynes was plain Yankee, the McGills, O'Hara and Sullivans were Irish and the Evans were Welch. To the west was a veteran freighter of the old Colville Trail, "Cap" Douglas, as solid a Scot as one could wish to meet. He often came to visit with William, and this was good, for strangely enough the latter was far from gregarious, despite early years amid teeming crowds of "rough-necks". That may have been the reason, for the less one dealt with such an element the better. Some three miles south lived the Bradburys, likewise on railroad land. The parents were immigrants from England near Tyne-mouth, and (the parents) had their way of talking, some of which carried over to the two daughters, Alice and Edith, and four sons, Ernest, Edward, Arthur and George, though all had some schooling and the normal Americanizing experiences to be absorbed at community gatherings. With them the sound of H was apt to show up where not needed and be dropped when called for in the usual pronunciation. Clara Abrams, too, retained certain mannerisms of speech, including that same tendency to misplace her 'aitches"; thus a boy named Art became Hart, and Harry would be 'arry. This occasioned no surprise where Irish brogue, Scottish burr, Yankee twang, German accents, and even a Southern drawl were often heard. She could speak to good purpose and sometimes there was no chance for the "English" to crop out. She loved to debate, and despite lack of formal education, had become well informed

Hay crop on recently broken sod.

on current happenings and versed in literature, thanks to their store of books, and thus a formidable advocate. Social gatherings at the school, and matters of public import, drew good representation from the surrounding territory. At the latter it was customary for the people to take turns in contributing to the enlightenment, for there was a serious purpose included underlying such get-togethers. There were recitations, discussions on current issues, skits, music and singing.

On one occasion a couple of young blades, somewhat the worse for the bottle, arose to supply their scheduled number. The offering continued until it verged on the "bawdy", and then went all out, so to speak. Strong men scowled and women hid their faces, but no hero arose to stop the affront. The young men were known to be prone to the use of knives and guns in disputes around home and here there were women and children to think of. Clara Abrams rose to her full height of 5 feet 2 inches, roused to righteous anger at seeing an activity dear to her heart thus profaned, and read the riot act to the culprits in a fashion that left them abashed and cringing. Such episodes were known to take place at community events but nothing similar ever happened again on that platform.

This episode gained for Mrs. Abrams a stature far beyond her inches but there was another arrow in the quiver. Neighborhood girls recounted with a touch of envy about the wonderful frocks the Abrams daughters wore to school and to socials. In time the young ladies became competent to assist in the sewing and do their share to keep up appearances. Manners and deportment were important and no chances were taken in their up-bringing. Life in crowded London had impressed Clara with the knowledge that there were people whose ways were not those of normal society. The home neighborhood numbered a few characters not to be trusted and so a close time check was kept to make sure there was no delay in returning from church or school. The wisdom of this later became apparent in a way to justify her strict attitude.

Truth to tell, Clara seemed to develop a rather jaundiced attitude regarding the role of wives and the menial status they were doomed to occupy. Once, when thoroughly "fed up," it took a five-mile walk toward Spokane to release her pent-up emotions and bring back the realization of how greatly she was needed. This helps understand why, years in advance of "Women's Lib," she was counseling the young ladies of her acquaintance that matrimony was not all "sunshine and roses." The effect of this lobbying is a matter of opinion. Her older daughters completed the usual eight years of schooling, enjoyed teenage popularity, then were gone. Lucy married Cyrus Payne who became a Spokane street and road contractor. Following her husband's death she managed the company and was a successful bidder for preliminary work at the Grand Coulee Dam site. Florence married Fred Hoefer, violinist and builder, and lived for some time on a timber claim near Coeur d'Alene prior to settling in Spokane. Bessie married John O. Chick, born in Chard, England, whose family came to Deep Creek Falls in the early 1880's. Both were ambitious to get a start in farming. They worked the land of her parents for several seasons, lived for a time in Spokane, and after 1921 owned their own diversified ranch at Nine Mile Falls. This left daughter Louisa, born in 1900, to attend a newer Greenwood School than her brothers and sisters had known, and help fill the void at home. She was graduated, then received instruction in high school subjects when enrollment was few, and a competent, interested teacher available. Her goal was business training.

Mrs. Abrams once endured "a five year stretch" without a shopping junket to "The Falls" so beyond doubt trips "to town" were always events to which the family could look forward with excitement. This was primarily due to the change of pace it offered for a twenty-mile drive behind a team had a certain monotony. The road left the prairie farm land and descended to the valley of Coulee Creek, then followed that indifferent stream, passing nothing of real interest save a sawmill and the home of Mr.

Changes were apparent on occasional trips to Spokan Falls.

and Mrs. George Pratt, at the Coulee Creek "crossing". Clara might have approved of Mrs. Amerella Pierce Pratt, niece of President Franklin Pierce, who conducted school classes and a postoffice in their modest home. Mrs. Pratt was an educated and liberated woman, which was all to the good, but her idea of freedom was expressed in marrying the man of her choice, George Pratt, an honest, highly skilled artisan. What the parents may have expected of this ambitious and talented daughter is a matter of conjecture but she never evinced any regrets and the community which became her "new home" was the better for her coming.

One day her educational efforts would be transferred to the Warsaw School, built by George Pratt on land donated by him, destined to also be the site of Farmers' Alliance meetings, literaries, political oratings, and Board of Directors' sessions.

The next and best place of all was the Seven-Mile Bridge over the Spokane River. Folks talked much of a gun battle there when a Sheriff's posse tangled with a group of drovers who were night-herding cattle. In those days buyers would start at Coulee City or thereabouts and head towards Spokane, purchasing along the way. Much of the land was open range and it was suspicioned that occasionally loose stock was "incorporated" in the herd destined for the slaughter house. Such thinking was back of the visit by the lawmen but the cowboys claimed they thought "rustlers" had jumped them. There were dead and wounded as an aftermath of the shooting, fuel for much talk in the grocery and feed stores.

The town of Spokan Falls had ceased to exist, largely turned to ashes in the fire of August, 1889. Now it was rebuilt and

The "new" Greenwood School later became a residence.

Posed beside this portable cook wagon are the competent cooks and a typical threshing crew of the early 1900's. Standing, John Chick is seventh from the left, and brother Arch is second.

improved with modern structures, known as Spokane, the hub of the "Inland Empire", the most important city in eastern Washington, this state also coming into existence in 1889. There were several railroads in addition to the remembered Northern Pacific. They entered town over spectacular steel trestles that bridged Hangman Creek or the river on the west. Sidewalks, paved streets, parks, industry, schools, department stores, hotels, restaurants, banks, streetcars, electricity and water under pressure together with indoor plumbing. There was much that represented improvement over even the London of Clara's girlhood, and this was worth consideration. The long journey homeward, often completed in the late hours, was a thing that began to pall. Electric trains that ran to so many of the country villages would certainly be a convenience, and there was talk of a dam being built north of home on the Spokane River that would generate a huge amount of electricity and be a very unique structure when completed. Better roads and the new-fangled automobiles that were beginning to make an appearance would make it easy to visit the Long Lake project and other points of interest in the near future.

William Abrams was reserved and preferred the companionship of his beloved books to exchanging small talk. He had been places and had seen things beyond the comprehension of his neighbors, but in significant matters their opinions were duly respected. One urged him to become an American citizen, pointing out the complications that otherwise impended for wife and children. It may have pleased him to be a lone symbol of the British Empire "on which the sun never set", but he could listen and think. Friends John H. Williams and E. W. McDowell witnessed his Certificate of Naturalization in 1894.

It is probable that to his acquaintances William Abrams appeared to be well off. If so it was because he had kept his hand on the plow and his nose to the grindstone, mindful perhaps of the Biblical admonition that man should live by the sweat of his brow. Thus he was very much a home body, one who enjoyed few familiar associations. In his absence, when folks "confabbed" together, there may have been references to "Bill" Abrams, or to "Old Man" Abrams, but when he was among them it was normally Mr. Abrams. This was due in part to advancing years, but primarily in recognition of his rather forceful and forthright personality, appropriate characteristics for a man determined and able to meet each and every responsibility, public or personal. In time that previously mentioned beard, crown of thick white hair,

Florence (Abrams) Hoefer and family pioneered this Idaho timber claim.

and frank, direct gaze, combined to give him the distinguished appearance artists so often portray when depicting the prophets and patriarchs of the Old Testament.

William Abrams cherished his hard won West Greenwood home.

How did he appear to his family? It is possible that as age made its inroads he may have seemed elderly indeed. Perhaps some of them wondered if it had been entirely proper for one of his experience to wed a wife much younger than himself and transport her in a series of wearying treks to this bleak outpost where everything had to be done the hard way. If such was the case an unprejudiced scanning of the surrounding families would have revealed many homes that were less fortunate. Nevertheless he was tested, and cruelly so.

Two baby daughters had died in infancy and death also claimed Percy at a tender age. The toil of establishing a productive estate would be for naught if the older boys chose to seek jobs in the "big city".

A Portland Oregonian news clipping came to hand reporting that his original mine in Abram's Gulch, Africa, had been sold once more, this time for 50,000 lbs, or $250,000 in money value of that time. The item was kept, and his comment remembered, "I guess the Lord didn't intend for me to be a rich man".

A truly tangible loss is described by Louisa. "Dad had gone into partnership with some neighbors in the purchase of a threshing machine. One year while they were threshing wheat on the home place the machine caught on fire, probably from a smut explosion. Florence and her five or six-year old son Wesley were visiting us at the time; and we had decided, along with mother, to have a look-see at operations when we saw flames shooting out of the blower and straw stack. Naturally we put on a burst of speed to get to the field, but by the time we arrived there was not much left. Nothing could be saved as there was no water on hand, except for the men's drinking needs, to put out the fire. It meant a great loss as I don't think there was any insurance to cover equipment or sacked grain. Just one more of the hazards of farming!"

Before barbed wire, fencing was a tedious task.

Indirectly, smut was again the villain when fate delivered the next low blow. While he was at work in the granary "dusting" seed to prevent smut in the next crop a vagrant swirl of air filled the eyes of Mr. Abrams with that potent and painful powder. Thereafter his eyesight failed rapidly. It must have been at about this time that he chose to gather his family and for the first time relate to them the complete chronicle of his earlier life. Perhaps he wanted a last chance to see the expression on his children's faces, to find if they saw in him anything but the work-worn parent they had always known. Actually two nights were required to complete the recitation and hopefully his faulty vision detected the show of interest he had wistfully desired. The interest was there but unfortunately no one recorded the saga in depth. Some colorful incidents were remembered; documents, pictures and heirlooms became keepsakes along with a few anecdotes committed to writing. Undoubtedly as many features of a marvelous story were lost as retained for when, in later years, as all too often happens, there was a wish to put it all together the recollections were hazy or subject to differing interpretations. With his devotion to literature Mr. Abrams should have kept a journal or diary, but in the beginning how could he have known that his career would follow an orbit far beyond the scope of the ordinary?

Louisa Abram's depicted ebb-tide in her father's career.

"Before Dad lost his sight entirely, he and brothers Bill and Walt played a game in which they used beans. I would hear them say words that sounded like "Auntie Bean". No doubt this was poker, (and the words meant ante a bean) but to an unsophisticated child it seemed a rather peculiar game they were playing. Later when the boys had left the farm to seek their fortunes———, Dad and I played Euchre and Seven-up until he was no longer able to distinguish the spots on the cards. Mother never cared for cards so Dad had to rely on me for playing.

"When he was no longer able to pursue his farming activities, he would go flower-picking with me in the spring. Also he invented

Young William Abrams, Army Engineers, World War I.

Walter Abrams, Infantry, World War I.

games with such characters as "Rosie Hornblower," and "Timothy Tug-mutton." I don't know just where he got these names (the Dickens' influence?), but they were amusing to a lonely child. As his sight steadily grew worse he was unable to go too far from the familiar environs of the home.

"We had an old horse called "Fatty" who was allowed to live out his remaining years in retirement. Somehow he seemed to sense that Dad was blind, for he would follow him around, carefully treading so he would not step on him. Dad would go to the carrot patch each day to pull up a few carrots and there would be Fatty waiting at the garden gate for his treat". Such faltering steps for a man who had trod the challenging terrain of five continents!

There was more to come. The United States entered World War I and sons Walter and Bill joined the Army. The youngest boy did not return from overseas. Things could never again be the same. Mrs. Abrams began to press for a move to Spokane since William could no longer do even the simplest of maintenance tasks. He resisted, wanting above all else to spend his last years in surroundings that were familiar. Once more Clara put her foot down, as she had done so long ago in Saskatchewan. "You can stay if you want to, but Louisa and I are moving to town".

This was no spur of the moment decision. In more than thirty years of concern for the community her interest in the well-being of its residents was recognized in the affectionate title "Auntie" Abrams. Her midwifery skills helped usher many a youngster into this world. Projects for the common good counted on her enthusiastic support. As a nurse she was the first resort, with a reputation for "keeping cool" in a crisis. This came by dint of harsh experience. As an illustration: during a childish scuffle between Walter and Bessie over who would drink out of a watering can, the girl ended up with a cut lip. In a first aid treatment, dictated by inspiration or desperation, the mother closed the gap by gluing a piece of cloth in place to draw and hold the cut edges together, and thus anticipated Band-Aids by many years. The exasperated father, fearing an ugly scar would result, exclaimed, "Why didn't you give them a loaded pistol to play with!"

West Greenwood School Picture, May 21, 1901.

Top row, left to right: Alice Williams, Nova Newlon, Elsie Newlon, Otto Nunn, Grace Puckett, Maude Lynch, Mayme Williams. Center: Josephine Rhodes, Zulu Nunn, Bessie Abrams, Bruce Shaw, Ray Whitman, Walter Abrams, Hugh Boyd, Herschel Shaw, Jessie Rhodes. Bottom: Mayme Judd, Evelyn Judd, Amanda Lehr, Bertha Lehr, unknown, George Williams, Timothy McGillicuddy, Will Williams. Teacher is Henry Gray.

What a relief when the injury healed so smoothly that only a faint trace could be detected by those who knew exactly where to look!

Stark tragedy occurred when two children, cousins, swallowed heart tablets left within reach. The call for help came but by the time the half-mile trip could be made a child had died. The father had administered emetics to one, who survived, but the mother and grandmother had been unable to compose themselves and cope, in the other instance. It was too late except to deal with the hysteria and help lay out the fatally stricken child for burial. Later another youngster from the same home with a fish hook lodged in one of his fingers was brought by the grandmother. The "nurse" solved this problem by wrapping string around the finger to temporarily numb it, and then removing the barb. Such a background of events posed considerable weight when pondering the problem of leaving, but the decision made, there was no turning back.

Reluctantly William recognized a certain wisdom in this, economically, aware that things would be easier for those of his family still about him. Clara would find city life more enjoyable than that on the farm, where his blindness had restricted activity. There would be advanced schooling for Louisa, and happily they might find a house that was not in need of constant repair. Inflated prices, incident to the wartime conditions rendered their property valuable beyond expectations. Wheat had reached $3.00 a bushel and predictions were it would never again go below that figure. The west 160, brought under cultivation in later years, sold on a contract for $7,200. The home place, more modestly priced, went for $5,530. Not exactly gold mining, perhaps, but all acquired while rearing a family and doing one's best for each member, and as honestly earned as anything that ever came his way.

The new home in Spokane was modest and well-built on west Spofford, and the years from 1918 to 1920 were ones free of labor.

No brother and sister were ever closer than Bessie and Walter.

It was easy for Clara to get "down town" and Louisa could train for secretarial work at one of the business colleges. William had much time to himself. Conceivably he mulled over the past, pondering where he might have taken a wrong trail. If so he should have gained much satisfaction from being true to the course he had chosen. Not inclined to retrospect, otherwise he would not have waited so long to relate the adventures of youth and early middle age, he must have sought to probe the future. Not too successfully it can be hoped, for there some disappointments might have been detected.

Oddly enough, not too far to the north in the Fort Colville-Toroda country, Ranald McDonald, America's own restless globe-trotter, and possible friend of Kalgoorlie days, spent his last years, but fortunately his wide roamings were carefully recorded. Even so, at that time he was as little known to fame as his English born contemporary.

With the passing of several decades certain changes would come to pass. All trace of the church and the Jimmy Jones store vanished and the weed-grown foundation of the "Abram's school" could be found only by one who knew precisely where to search. All of the buildings erected at so much expense and labor deteriorated to a few decayed boards that will soon merge with the soil, and rusted nails that will leave little for even a metal detector to discover. A couple of shallow pits mark the house and cool storage, and even the spring's fresh flowing has been curtailed. Some of the mighty pines through which the wind soughed with a melody not always soothing have crashed to earth and no busy hands have been there to cut them into firewood, trim the hedge or prune the fruit trees.

There was so little left that Mr. Abrams could do; sit in a chair with one of his books, identified by touch, and recall its contents. The house was often quiet. Louisa was in school, and later employed in a bank at Harrington, Washington.

Clara adapted well to city life and was unawed by the new environment. She campaigned and petitioned for neighborhood improvements, sewers, sidewalks, streets and lighting. There were 35 years in hinterland "backwaters" to compensate for now with shows, libraries, restaurants and increased acquaintances. Excellent and economical streetcar transportation always provided regular mobility. Three married daughters lived in or near Spokane and there were several grandchildren entitled to a generous share of recognition and attention; Lillian, Pauline and Cyrus Payne, Wesley, Clara and Fred Hoefer, William, Carl, Clyde, Edna and Walter Chick. Her activities provided fuel for conversation and visitors brightened some days, but the husband was a man whose temperament did not adjust easily to the enforced idleness that preceded his death in 1920 at the age of 84.

Clara Abrams made a long-anticipated return to England during 1922. In London she sought vainly for members of her family. Failing to find any sisters was not too disappointing as their married names were not known to her. The name Ciff was found on a few tombstones but why was it missing from all the directories? There had been boys. In less than 40 years had they all died, moved to other cities, or like herself, emigrated to distant lands? The Capital on the Thames ceased to charm; her strength and time were insufficient for a more thorough search of church and cemetery records, and a shocking finality punctured all her hopes.

A few years later, in 1930, Mrs. Abrams was enrolled a Gold Star Mothers' excursion to France. For 800 *years* men of English blood, including kinsmen, had served and died on that alien soil. Standing at her son's grave she realized Walter was numbered in those ranks. In the 20th Century an ocean and a broad continent had provided no insulation from Europe's endless round of troubles—and untimely death. Did she forsee three grandsons being called to the colors "next time?"

Though six children reached adulthood there are none of the younger generation who perpetuate the Abrams name. Only surviving son, Bill, settled at Coeur d'Alene, Idaho, with his wife, formerly Mrs. Mame Rink, and her two sons. There are descendents by other names, however, to carry on certain traits of their forebearers; industry, integrity, loyalty, ambition and independence.

Back home at West Spofford she resumed her city routine, with a complication added. That west quarter section, sold on contract when wheat was $3.00 a bushel, reverted back when "things leveled off" and the purchaser "couldn't make it". There

S. S. "PRESIDENT ROOSEVELT"

This ship carried Clara Abrams to France in 1930.

went a goodly portion of the livelihood and it became necessary to find renters, sometimes via an agent. After that happened months passed "waiting for the harvest" in hopes the income would cover fees, taxes, and allow a bit extra. Under these conditions being responsible for management was a trial, and the coming of "The Depression" made it a burden. In some years the 160 acres from which much had been expected was really a Jonah, though not one to cast overboard just yet.

Fortunately there was a positive viewpoint for persons blessed with a modicum of security and discernment. Because in youth her own education had been severely limited Clara was an ardent admirer of America's Public Schools. She sat for a photograph in 1929, backed by Freddy Hoefer, Cyrus Payne, William and Carl Chick, proud of these grandsons who attended Spokane's North Central High School. Their youthful training was not being stinted, bad as the times were.

Louisa's progress in the business world brought about a return to Spokane, and then a transfer to Seattle, an opportunity her father could not have visualized 50 years earlier. Clara joined her there and found the city more than a fulfillment of earlier predictions. William had twice circled the globe; she had completed a smaller orbit and was content back on Puget Sound in the land of big trees. Her role in life had been a demanding one, performed with competence against an often somber background. This new stage was attractive. She enjoyed those fresh surroundings where in 1884 she had been ready to spend a lifetime, until her death in 1931.

Though six children reached adulthood there are none of the younger generations who perpetuate the Abrams name. There are descendants by other names, however, to carry on certain traits of their forbears; industry, integrity, loyalty, ambition and independence.

When William Abrams brought his family to Spokan Falls he made the hard choice of electing to wrest a living from a farm on the tough frontier sod instead of gambling on the future at Prichard Creek's gold diggings, or following the rush to stake one of Coeur d'Alene's bountiful lodes of *silver*. He should have had no regrets. In the long run much that was good came to pass, and in his own being there were so many of the qualities that will always be labeled— —Sterling.

Clara Abrams with four grandsons then enrolled at North Central High School in 1929. Left to right, Fred Hoefer, Cyrus Payne, William Chick, Carl Chick.

Gold Star Mothers at the Oise-Aisne American Cemetery in France. Clara Abrams, second from the left, front row.

Lucy (Abrams) Payne in her Coeur d'Alene Park apartment.

Teacher Henry Gray's remembrance to each West Greenwood student.

Seldom did the surviving brother and his sisters enjoy a "get together" but this 1938 photo shows all of them, left to right, Louisa, Bessie, William, Florence and Lucy.

Log cabin featuring roof made of hand riven shakes.

Army of the United States of America

To all who shall see these presents, greeting:

This is to certify that

WALTER W. ABRAMS

Private 1st Class, Company M, 23rd Infantry

died with honor in the service of his country

on the twenty-second day of July, 1918.

Given at Washington, D.C., office of The Adjutant General of the Army,

this twenty-second day of November, one thousand nine hundred and eighteen.

Adjutant General.

Confirmation of Walter Abram's death in World War I.

Winter was often a frigid, forbidding season.

The Government of the United States
extends an invitation to
Mrs. Clara Abrams
to make a pilgrimage to the
Cemetery in Europe where the remains of her
Son are now interred
Leaving New York on the
Steamship Roosevelt,
on May 28, 1930.

This communique insured Clara's second mission to France.

During inclement weather the Abrams home seemed isolated.

After years of hoping, in 1930 Clara visited Walter's grave.

Th

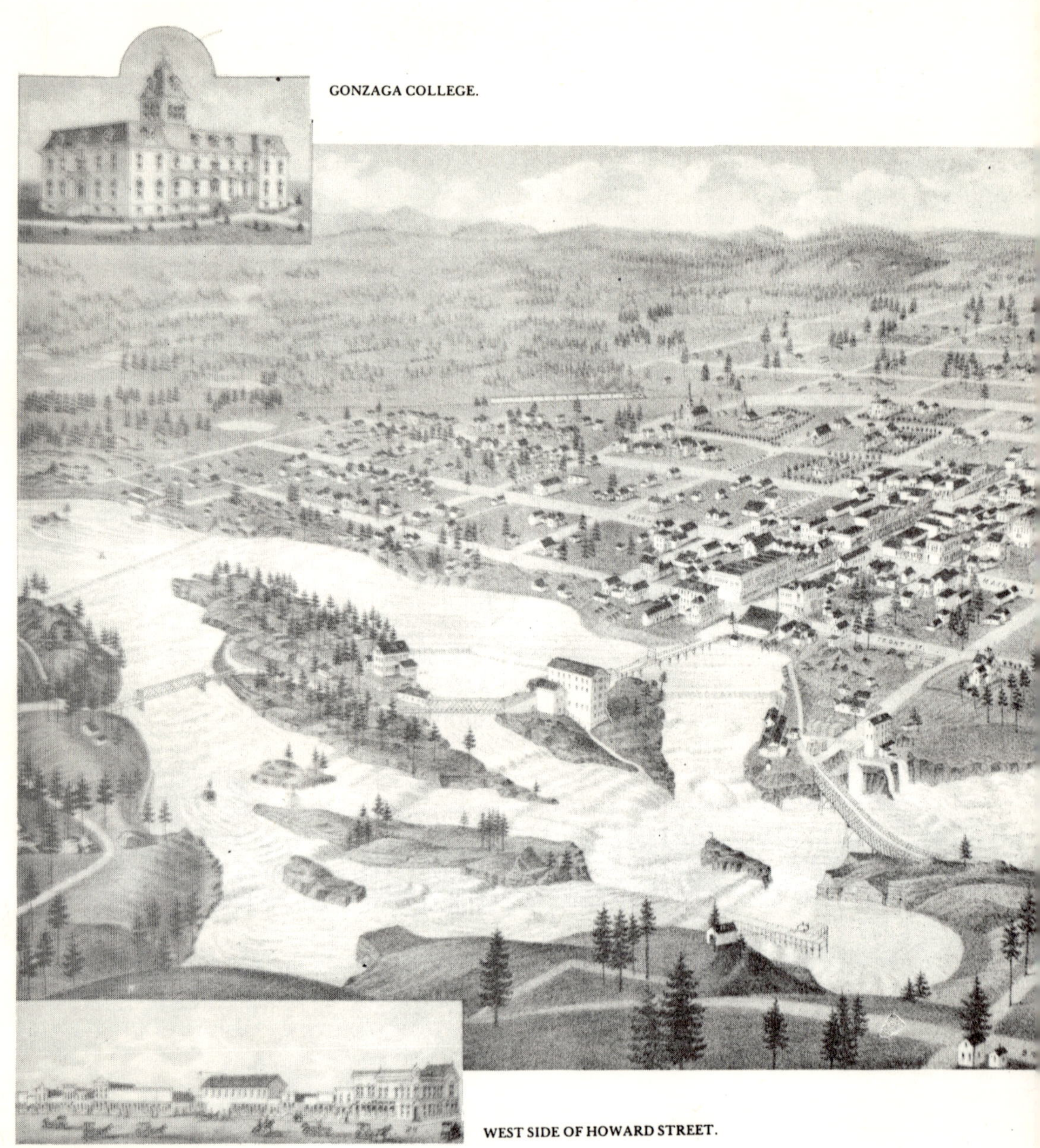
GONZAGA COLLEGE.

WEST SIDE OF HOWARD STREET.

SPOKAN FALLS, WASHI